Sam C   ). Armagh, in 1936
and ha   ʾ for the past thirty
years. Apart from four years compiling and editing the *Poet's Yearbook*, and occasional bouts of freelance journalism and reviewing, his working life has been spent in architecture.

PROTESTANT WINDOWS

PROTESTANT WINDOWS

SAM GARDINER

LAGAN PRESS
BELFAST
2000

Acknowledgement is due to the following magazines for first publication of a number of the poems: *Ambit, The Guardian, London Magazine, New Statesman, Nova Poetica, The Observer, Poetry London, Poetry Review, The Rialto, Rivet.* 'Protestant Windows' won first prize in the 1993 National Poetry Competition.

Published by
Lagan Press
7 Lower Crescent
Belfast BT7 1NR

ARTS
COUNCIL
of Northern Ireland

ISBN: 1 873687 32 X

Author: Gardiner, Sam
Title: Protestant Windows
2000

Cover Design: Cushnahan Design Services
Set in Palatino
Printed by Noel Murphy Printing, Belfast

for Eileen

CONTENTS

NOT AT HOME

On belonging and being tired of it,
of having to stay and change the world
or stay the world and change, I broke
away to the time-out of crowds.

Twelve months in London and I began
commuting by way of Trafalgar Square
to visit my father's pigeons, the ones
he waited for on a distant hillside.

Eyes peeled skywards for specks
barely moving above blue trees,
loaded shotgun against the fence
for pigeon-fancying peregrines,

he waited long weekends for pigeons
who stayed away instead of homing in
on that stifling, hawk-eyed pigeon loft
in an endless drift of open fields.

Who said, 'This world is not our home'?
I forget, but he was right; as you are
when you leave a message complaining
that I'm never at home. I never was.

ASHES TO ASHES

Seagoe Churchyard is the last place
you want to be, so I went there first,
drove straight from the airport
past the same lowing, mudcaked
cattle country seen each day
from the black-windowed London tube.

Too late, except for those regrets
called memories, but there's one thing
he might like and understand, strictly
between ourselves. Twenty-one years
and not forgotten, not for a minute.
Gets closer, in fact.

                And only the father
knows why the son came so far
with nothing to give, no flowers,
no headstone cleaner, no tears,
to stand there alone in the stillness
and smoke ten Woodbine over his grave.

SHOT

A lead sinker glinting on the tow-path
sparked off a flashback to that evening
between homework and bed. The shotgun ogled
from all angles, oiled and polished like new,

I was allowed to aim it at the open fire,
squint one-eyed down the bore of each barrel
into the spinning flames, before aligning
the heavy halves, struggling till they locked.

Those oily pull-throughs I understand,
but was it graphite that greased the moving parts,
lampblack, soot, or some concoction of your own?
Fathers always die before you think to ask them.

Mum had been reading how, in miracle plays,
Adam and Eve sometimes trod the boards
white-leathered from head to toe for naked.
My father leapt a hedge and got the picture:

500 Norton parked round the back, he grinned,
moving from the big pine table, scrubbed
till the grain rippled, towards a winter evening
gazing into the fire, inventing television.

What they were unaware of, and I remember,
was the pellet of lead shot I had fished from
the rabbit stew, clicking against my teeth
for sucking later, like some adult sweet.

I NEVER THANKED YOU FOR

: giving me life, giving me death;
the dog and gun days;
the time you spent making box-kites
that got away;
the mushrooming before breakfast;

showing me the ropes
for hauling bales of linen and binding corn;
the bible-beltings
and the wrongs that were good for me
(I miss them);

the games of draughts you lost on purpose,
and the fights you won
in Sunday kitchens full of loud,
blue-chinned, argumentative uncles;
the big hand at school prizegivings

and for being twice the man
that Colin Medlow's father was,
and Errol Furst's, and Charlie McCreedy's;
sparing the rod
when I paddled across the flooded quarry
in a waterlogged wardrobe;

no living daylights beaten out of me,
of course I did it again, am still doing it.
And I never thanked you for suddenly
dying
to show me how it's done.

CACTUS

First sign of spring, first blush
and the desert rangers
rush your self-addressed postcard,
'Hurry on over!' No excuses,
not now that air-conditioning
has opened up the desert,
but you'd better skip work
tomorrow or the furnace blast
will have set the spiny succulents
hissing and spitting dried flowers.

The fifty-gallon barrel cactus
now bristling between the rocks
will lose its crown of rosebuds:
desert has the last word.
Or drop in by default—I admit it—
and catch, over there, behind the hot
creosote bushes, the oval platters
of the bandit-sized prickly pear
artlessly fringed with marigolds.

In Ulster (a province now opened up
by intermittent wipe) the desert's
diminutives in tiny plastic pots
fill a window sill in a nursing home
for incontinent widows, who never
dreamt they would come to this.
Spring has no place, no season
where those prickly captives, barrels
and pincushions refuse to spike
the disinfected air with blossom.

Lined up, they make a stockade
behind which my mother pries on
the daily comings and goings,
and beyond which Craigavon Hospital

[15]

rears its gravestone slabs;
while here, the cinder-blue sierra
distantly rides the haze. I send her
a picture postcard: 'from my cacti
to yours', between deserts.

RIP MRS. FARQUHAR RIP

Mrs. Farquhar was a gnarled, irascible recluse
when I was 12, and no older twenty years later
when she was taken away, presumably to die. But
if you are still alive, Mrs. Farquhar, and reading this,
you will see that the lad you always knew would come
to a bad end is declining nicely.
No one knew your story, or needed to. Yesterday's
stories were like that, but today, today was different.

Alone in her two-storey family home, monkey-puzzle
at the front and five or six apple trees (Beauties of Bath,
delicious) round the back, Mrs. Farquhar spent her days
knitting socks for her war-dead sons. We sniggered
behind her back, never to her scarlet face
and knobbly walking stick. 'There will always be wars
and rumours of wars,' she would assert, shaking her stick
and clearly prepared to start one single-handed.

She spoke with awesome authority
on the Black Death and the Great Potato Famine,
having survived both, apparently.
And she remembered 1641 as if it were yesterday:
the massacre of Protestants on the bridge in Portadown.
Sluggish with the corpses of settlers
from Worcestershire, the river slowly twisted and turned
red. The sky flowed white and blue.

The Passed On were more real than the Still Here,
and when I raided her little orchard until she gave me
sixpence to pull the ripe apples and store them in trays
in her shed, she was saving bygones, not apples.
One of the new, everything goes, know-alls, I waved
(slightly) when the Queen drove past the end of the lane
and loitered not seen to be listening when de Valera
grieved from the back of a coal lorry in Union Street.

Mrs. Farquhar lived in other times, we told one another. Until the killing started. Distant relatives, we assumed they were relatives so distant she had written them off, took her away and the house stood empty. Somehow, Beauties of Bath lost their flavour.

RIP, Mrs. Farquhar, and congratulations—you were right. But apologies if you are still with us, which I suspect you are. In fact, the evidence is overwhelming.

PROTESTANT WINDOWS

They come at sunset peddling daylight, two
salesmen wearing glasses, through which they view
his shabby sliding sashes with disdain.
'Wood?' they suppose and feign
dismay. 'Yes, comes from trees,'
and he raises the drawbridge ten degrees,
a hurdle to reservists
but child's play to front-line evangelists
with news of paradise
on earth (at this address to be precise)
in whitest white PVC.
                              'Think of all
the blessings. And if economical
heavenly comfort isn't what you need,
think of Our Earth,' they plead,
and their plastic-rimmed, double, glazed eyes glow
with love for generations of window
salesmen as yet unborn. 'If I were you,
I'd save my CO_2
for atheists and papists. I doubt
they even know about
King Billy.' 'Who?' 'William III to you,
brought sliding sashes to
Britain, fetched in pure air and sanity.
Without him we'd still be
in the dark.'
                              'Sorry, we must go. It's late,'
they say, and beat a retreat to the gate,
and pause. Quick as a flash
he raises an effortlessly sliding sash
for a parting shot. 'Plastic heretics!'
he shouts. The window sticks.

He tugs, a sash-cord snaps, the window drops
on his head, where it stops.
Latimer and Ridley know how he feels

as bloodied, martyred for his faith, he reels
towards eternity,
where planets, the latest novelty,
are looking less and less
like being a success.

THE HOME FRONT

Night before the mourning after they sing
of Ire Land, my gnomeland. Kevin Barry
would not be proud of them, a tall at all,
in the King's Head abroad in Camden Town.
But Orangemen and their lemans out on a limb
in Ulster (twinned with Serbia) know that when
Irish eyes are smiling you hit the deck,
slither for cover and ease your ghost-making
357 Magnum from its holster.

BLESSED OLIVER
after Milton's 'To the Lord General Cromwell'

Cromwell, chief, new foes arise, old friends
Among them, traitors you would recognize
Despite their blarney and comical disguise,
But we were too obsessed with making amends
For old mistakes, going south for weekends,
Too buttered with welcome to realize
What black depths they would plumb to colonize
Our British home. Their guile is what offends,
Their condoning murder to further their ends,
But the spirit of Cromwell never dies;
It gives us strength. No one can terrorize
Those who fear only God; our Faith defends
Us from a more impressive wrath. Now go,
Go in peace, but not at any price:
The time for bravery and sacrifice
Is when Evil crawls out and begins to crow
And strut about. You won't have far to search:
Collect your handguns as you leave the church.

GOOD DOG
In 1722, the rector of Drumcree, Dr. Tisdall, received his old
acquaintance, Dean Swift.

Protestant dogs are loyal, too loyal
for those they are loyal to, and lovable,
but when attacked tend not to mince their words,
just the shanks of their critics. Guard-dogs,
guide-dogs and underdogs by nature,
they are distressed to have to bludgeon re-
publicans and sinners to death with their tails
when the democratic process fails.
Protestant dogs once roamed the British Isles
sniffing out incense, false ideals, idols,
sacramental sex complete with penance
and all the purgatorial nonsense
dished out by Rome. Now penned in Ulster, they roam
unnerved and only feel at home at home.

Protestant dogs, who enjoy a direct
line to God (they ring on Sundays, cheap rate),
weep for their priest-ridden neighbours, but some
people you just can't help—damnation suits them.
Protestant dogs, though menaced on one side
by a tagged rabble of Gaels, wild with greed,
and on the other by an avalanche
of backsliding Saxons, give not an inch
but march the streets in the rain, up and down,
playing silver flutes, rattling drums for crown
and country, out of step but not caring,
up and down in the rain, not surrendering.

A van parks in Portadown, Market Street,
packed with explosive. In the passenger seat
a Protestant dog, a golden retriever, completes
the ideal family as he waits. And waits.
'Good dog,' the policeman says, trying
the door handle in vain. Then comes the warning.

The bomb destroys a dozen shops. The dog
is blown to bits, vanishes in a red fog.
The RSPCA decline to comment.
The Kennel Club are unmoved, they resent
an ancient pedigree which reaches back
through Calvin and Wyclif to Noah's Ark.
Blown-up, talked down, Protestant dogs don't shrink;
they are too busy being not extinct.

IN THE BIRD HIDE

One place he hadn't been, though the brochures
said Don't miss it, was Oxford Island
which is not an island, not in Lough Neagh.
A grey Sunday could-be-anywhere place
of damp grass and miles of land and water
flattened by gravity, dipping birds doubling
for dinosaurs the only signs of life.
Intrigued by a bird hide beside the water,
a hushed hut on stilts, Robert eased himself
up the steps like a trespasser.
Inside, a bulky ornithologist
with hedgehog hair and steady binoculars
stared hard at the water.
This was serious. Had it not been for the hearty
if belated, 'Come in, there's lots of room'
he would have sloped off to admire the reeds
which could well be rushes.
The slotted view from the hide, in its linearity
like that enjoyed from a tank,
had kept him curious for all of two minutes
when anonymous birds began receiving names
from the watcher, who recognised a spectacled
oaf when he saw one. Raising his binoculars
for a better look at moorhen, water rail or coot
his sleeve fell back to reveal,
high up on the back of his wrist,
a small red *US* tattooed. For Robert,
first American holiday booked, and eager
for the okay from an evident devotee,
this was all the excuse he needed.
'United States?' he volunteered, glancing
pointedly at the now retracted clue.
The twitcher laughed. 'No, Ulster Separatists:
always two moves ahead. Have you noticed
the great crested grebes? Here, take a look,'
binoculars thrust out lens first and heavy,

the twin grey barrels warm from his hands.
'Separatists?' Robert mumbled apologetically,
scanning the dazzling drizzle
before focussing on what he thought must be
a crestfallen grebe treading water.
'Here on holiday, are you?' the birdwatcher
enquired. This could be a problem.
'No, I live here now.' 'Not long, I think.
Not long enough to understand.'
'Well, I've been here three years. How long
does it take?' 'Oh, four hundred years or so.'
Robert, no expert on birds either, always careful
not to interfere with nature (no loud noises,
no sudden movements), retreated
with footsteps as light as feathers.

REINCARNATION

Being a Buddhist was difficult
in the hodgepodge of country lanes
on my new Lambretta: such a dithering
scatter of short, consecutive lives,
ex-people with wings in commotion
between the hedges, rabbits refusing to stand

aside. A broken wrist and, worse,
bent forks from avoiding a head-on
collision with a large blue butterfly—
which God alone witnessed (I hope),
and must have sent—expunged the heresy.

If all the nicer people I have been
could see me now, opening the garage
this unclouded morning,
they would disown me, scrubbing
the speckled blood from the windscreen.

ROOK

A fight in the sky, a furious, harsh tangle
of wings, beaks, claws, and accusations,
and a rook plunges for sanctuary
into the tree above the Wesleyan chapel,
leaving a few black feathers riding the air.
Three rooks flap raggedly off, but return
outraged at intervals throughout the afternoon,
sending the outcast ducking and dodging
among the twigs. Lodged there for the best part
of a week, he has taken to haranguing
all sinners within earshot, of whom there are
a few, enslaved by vanity, the world,
the flesh, and the devil. They will repent
and mend their ways, by God, or croak in Hell.
The chapel has been silent for more than
twenty years, and our best-kept village
hasn't suffered such an upset since
John Wesley preached here in 1756.

NO TITLE

There are things we need words for,
like enamel jug, buttercups, crusty loaf,

and things we don't, such as love,
subatomic particles, that shooting star,

and there are words we need things for, God,
for example, ghosts, the verse in the universe.

But nothing needs words for us,
no thing looks us up in books and thinks,

How interesting, I must look out for one.

SANITY TABLETS

Ghosts? No problem. We've got pills for phantoms.
I find chlorpromazine (only 40p
for twenty) useful for treating symptoms
like yours. Side effects? Rare, but apathy,

impotence and death have been noted. Still,
I wouldn't worry; strength of dose depends
on whether your spooks are as quick to kill
as, for instance, imaginary friends.

You have principles? I see, Apparitions
debase religion, mock the spiritual?
OK. Let's have no more visions or Virgins
and you can forget angels on the steeple.
Take these pills: become one of the reasons
why ghosts no longer believe in people.

SEASONAL GREETINGS

Two brothers, from their red-gold curls,
aged eight and nine at a guess, Robin
Goodfellow times two, are scouting
the Saturday malls for someone
to administer their daily scare.

Having picked their Humpty-Dumpty,
soft-boiled, middling plump, benign and
minding his wife's green shopping bag
outside The Body Shop, they get set
and start, not with 'Ring a ring o' roses',

far less 'You spotted snakes with double
tongue', but with *You dirty paedophile!*
in shrill trebles, *You dirty paedophile!*
Pink and quick they dance back, taunting,
You touched me, you dirty paedophile!

Flushed, strangling with wrath, he stumbles
towards them. They separate and fly
hey diddle diddle among the dawdlers
with a parting *Dirty paedophile!*
and are swallowed down by the motley.

Humpty clings dizzily to the wall
and watches the precinct tilt and begin
to rock, gently, up and down, up
and down farther and farther, the lights
capsizing towards blackness.

All right, mate? Steady. Need any help?
No, no. And he retraces his steps
one by one by one to where his wife
is clutching the green shopping bag,
and anxiously scanning closed faces.

[31]

A coffee later he catches sight
of his accusers in one of the valleys
of toys ranged for Christmas, kneeling
innocent before anthropomorphic
Furies from other sad planets.

EASY INSTALMENTS

When he was ten and dying was what pets
and uncles did, he fancied being slain
in single combat on a thundering plain
complete with tors, as in film sets,

rather than keeling over in the straw
for no good reason. But at twenty
it would be death by love. Definitely.
Confused by infidelity and warts

he stalled, turned tail and raised the tempo
to a scream of speed in most directions,
envisaging spectacular collisions
and death by thirty. What a way to go.

Forty years young. He still had time
to die frozen deep inside a glacier,
where incredulous medics would discover
him centuries hence, in his prime.

Fifty, and it was getting rather late
to find a cause worth dying for, but he
might be persuaded. It would be
in public on a momentous date.

Drunk at sixty, and the mottled beast
which had dogged him down the years drew near.
He raised his glass to it, received no answer.
Birthdays found him not at his best,

though sixty-one came quite close to the mark.
His least ignominious endings all
conjoined when, in a drunken brawl
with his ex-wife in an icy car park

on Friday December the 31st,
he slipped and fell, cracking his head
on a concrete bollard, and was pronounced dead
by an off-duty chiropodist.

Best thing was, he says, his life in flashpast
as he fell, the deeds of his own instruction
laid out stone-cold for inspection.
Sudden death, he thinks, has drawbacks. At last

he's one of us, determinedly hanging on
to settle up by slow, bite-sized instalments,
fighting, losing limb by limb and sense by sense,
until what's left goes looking for what's gone.

WATER CONTENT

Like that last glass of brandy
you were 71 per cent water.
Your dying was less a question
of earth to earth than water to water,
and a five gallon cloud
shadowing the cemetery.

Apart from the one bank holiday
when rain danced, thunder clapped
and you leapt puddles like a clown,
there were no clouds in Woking
when I came visiting, or if there were
I never noticed them.

Back in London I took to stretching out
on the floor between sink and fridge
and scaling the chimneys opposite
into a private box of sky.
Many a time I saw you drifting by.

Today in Lincolnshire I watch
white cryogenic cirrus
at 40,000 feet sailing east
with grey cumulus blustering west
through the trees. So many of you,
I hadn't realised.

I'm glad you're not alone. Everyone
who has ever given up the ghost—
whether or not they had a ghost to give—
is there, recycling in the sky,
turning to icy pebbles, rain, dew,
singing in the bathroom plumbing.

Like that last glass of brandy,
the one you flushed the pills down with

(sent home with prostate cancer
and enough painkillers to last you
the rest of your life), the world
is 71 per cent tears,
water, rain-clouds, tears again.

TENNIS
at Thornton Abbey, Lincolnshire

Never so glad to see the star as now,
knackered at dusk and bored with tossing Mack
the sheep-thief in a tarpaulin, the shepherds
chorus 'Amen. Let's go.' *Puer natus est.*
The pageant cart, wheels stuck in muddy ruts
crisping to a mash of ice, transfers them,
courtesy of the Guild of Smiths and Wrights,
partying to Bethlehem. A swig of malmsey
and Abbot William nods approval
from his oriel window.

           Splendid, he nods again:
most important of the five senses is
the sense of wonder. And it could be worse:
'Joseph's Doubts About Mary,' for example;
too near the knuckle, with an uptight peasantry
and the lanes crawling with left-wing gospellers
in trendy rags. Blue against the cart's red
and gold wainscot, Mary cradles her bairn.

The first shepherd has brought a bob of cherries,
the second swings a bird in a wicker cage,
the third, 'It breaks my heart to see you here
so poorly clad and penniless,' hands Him
a ball. 'Now run and play, Lord,' he urges,
'Play tennis.' Tennis? Of course, tennis; John Ball
the rebel priest! The penny drops; every eye
stares up defiantly. The abbot stiffens
to just another stony effigy.

           The abbey's great
oak gates that creaked shut against torched nights
and pitchfork men now hang insensibly agape.
Adults £1.60, children 80p. Winter opening:
weekends 10 till 4. From across the fields,

15 tons of fuel, 30 tons of metal and 60
Smiths and Wrights soar skywards, rotating beacon
pulsing a quick string of stars, bound for Christmas in Tenerife. *Puer natus est.*

PRINCIPIA POETICA

This is Lesson 3 of 12. Let us start
high on the left and step down line by line.
The page must be held at an angle, thus,
the top farther away, the bottom nearer
so that it points directly at the heart.
The poem will advance down the incline
towards you as you read, the added impetus
assisting progress towards and by the reader.

Come into the sun. Watch it move from left
to right—the sun, not the poem. Look round:
your shadow also moves left to right
and the pen's natural path is demonstrated.
Antipodean poets often felt
hemispherically challenged and, having found
they had to view life through their legs to write
like Europeans, upped and emigrated.

Poems are not built upwards from the ground
like summer-houses, hotels and pagodas.
These are heavily built, stage upon stage.
Words however are lighter than air
and have to be caught in flight and pulled down.
The story of upward writing as good as
proves the case. Go to the foot of the page;
write upwards, piling lines above each other.

Quiet! Now, note these inky smudges and scuffs
where, alas, you sullied the line below.
Scribes who wrote this way were finally demoted,
heavily fined, and berated by their wives
for coming home from work with ink-stained cuffs.
Poetically, downwards is the way to go.The next lesson,
Lesson 4, is devoted
to feet, and why they must march past in fives.

HALF-A-MILE FROM HOME

Returning gone eleven after a day
at the Poetry Library, the London coach
set me down outside St. Michael & All Angels,
less than half-a-mile from home,
and died away. A young man
(answering the usual police description
of someone's son) overtook me, shouldering past
on the empty footpath.
Look out! I thought, or up! suddenly dependent
on a sky friend looking down.
Some twenty yards or so ahead, he stopped
and turned. 'What are you looking at?
Have you a problem?' he demanded.
'No,' I lied, warily avoiding the clash of eyes.
'I'll stab you,' he said flatly.
A few more steps and I pushed through the gate
of a house in darkness.
He hung back, watched me
walk up some stranger's private path
jingling my keys and, for my closing trick,
putting one to the door lock. He kicked the fence,
spat scathingly and went. Nobody told me
that being a poet was so dangerous.

FALL OF THE CARDS

Loose with elsewhereness, I stray towards
the card shop—greetings cards for all occasions—
and join the glad cascade of faces
on the escalator, where a fountain droops
into a cobalt pond and children drop coins
to the gods of the place.

                    Overwhelmed by aisles
of tiered wishes, folded cardboard prayers,
from *On Your Sad Bereavement*
to *Happy Xmas to My Car*, I signal
distress. What I need, not complaining,
is a card that says, quite simply,

Dear Sylvia, sorry to hear you have
inoperable cancer of the pancreas.
Get well soon. Playful among blonde bears
and silver horseshoes, two young
not yet shop-soiled assistants bend

obligingly over bottom drawers,
delicate fingers delving and wide red lips
looking up. Not a pancreas between them.
How about *Sorry You're Leaving Us*
or this one, *It Won't Be the Same Without You*?

All but done with making do, playing
the losing hands continually dealt her, Sylvia
(59) is dying down, for the first time ever
mown by passing years, and hoping not
to rise again, except vertically.

                    Meanwhile,
she sleeps and wakes with morphine smiles
in her bedroom across the road, now lit all evening,
the downstairs lying dark and empty. Thank you;
I'll take *Congratulations on Passing Your Test*,
and *Good Luck in Your New Home.*

FLIGHT

'Go,' she pleaded, 'I'll be fine,' head flung
forward, pale beneath soft brown hair.
He kissed the nape of her neck, bent over
the string of bright red gemstones, and left:
some days made more sense from the air.
But the time-shared Cessnas were lined up,
lashed down trembling, grounded by
a thunderstorm astride the runway.

At walking speed the anvil-topped pillar
salvoed and trampled west, high on ice
and electricity, the central downburst
fanning out in gusts which suddenly switched
from an eight-knot tail wind to fifty knots on
the nose. What can you do? Accelerate
and overshoot? Brake and pancake? Or
risk your fuel reserves and circle, and circle?

And he remembered the electrons crackling
as he combed them out of her hair
at bedtimes. I'd rather die, she had smiled.
He blamed St. Paul, blamed him a lot
for that 'woman's hair is her glory' shit.
Enter skinhead girl, pilot's licence still wet.
Exit bearded a small bald saint with big ideas.
Secretly nursing a lock of woman's hair?

'Keep your chemotherapy and,' the trade-off,
'I'll keep my hair.' Throttle open, tunnelling
the wind and easing back the wheel he rose
above the bleached and flattened abbey and
(Black Death/white death) the Killingholme
oil refineries' tall, silver chimneys,
one wearing a necklace of red lights.
Every dying day she combs her hair.

Climbing, wings rocking over billows
and empty pockets of air, levelling off
a mile below high curls and kisses of cloud,
he radioed for clearance to climb 3,000
feet and, drowning upwards in the sky,
cursed each and every one of the 3,000
times he had meant it when he said,
'Your hair looks very nice, love. Beautiful.'

INSTEAD OF RAIN

Instead of rain, April snow
infiltrated the orchard. She rang
to let him know, the pain spiralling,
trembling down the cable,

and caressed a telephone
which rang 300 miles away six months ago.
When he answered they spoke of
climatic change, the price of cut flowers
(How would he know a thing like that?)
and wasn't it a shame that Eve had failed
her test again, of any/everything
but love, or whatever it was
that hurt those parts of her that wanted him.
The stained-glass saints on the landing melted
and streamed away as she breathed.

Last time he came, michaelmas daisies
were burning like tiny gas-rings,
the lanes were wild with garlic
and holding him close she had felt
his boil-in-the-bag heart lurching madly
inside his shirt the colour of steam.
Faithful to the touch, but not beyond arm's length.
But she had never really liked his eyes,
either of them. Or his hair, hairs. As for the sweat
his balding head had dripped on her breast
and then his conceited spine buttoned up
against her, well, forgiving evil was easier.

Old woollen coat, rank with musk,
heavy with pollen, around her shoulders
she stands in the snow orchard,
among the powdered branches
and last year's rotten apples,
surprised by the first hint of blossom.

THE OLD SHRUBBERY

He liked it best when, on warm afternoons,
she wheeled him past the broken urns
and parked him beside the rhododendrons.
Dying is easier among ruins,
and history helps, a good degree
in sharing supper with one's ancestry,
and being misjudged.
                        The right posterity
never comes. His carer would disagree.
'Just count your blessings,' she would say. He did,
all 32 of them. The thirty-third
flapped its great wings above his head.

Ordered to let the sunshine do him good,
he turned his inquisitorial stare
on his disappointing daughter
(old habit, looking for what wasn't there)
but saw few people now. She would sooner
open a coffin than a book,
and now hung over him, philanthropic
to a fault. A dull woman. His mistake.
'Call me when you like.'
                        Yes, to stack him back
among his books, with the rare editions
well out of reach, many with broken spines
from spirited reading between the lines,
to be with friends when it happens.

But sunlight (this with grudging approval)
was improbably beautiful,
the sky a deep, unforgivable blue
and holly confiding its tiny blooms.

'... FOR WINNING LOVE WE WIN THE RISK OF LOSING'
—Thomas Hardy

Subterfuge brought me your address,
and no, I shan't stage protests
to affront your portico.
What do I want? The sun and moon.
When do I want them? Soon.
What else do I want? An adjournment;
I want to celebrate this longing.

Served with formal notice to quit,
my longing quitted not. I moved out
without it, as I thought, but when I tried
to shake it off at 95 along the M180,
the farmers were spraying their crops
with rainbows and my longing
overtook me on the inside lane.

Bad day, goodnight. Bent on lifting
my mind off my mind,
I subside slowly bone by bone, organ
by organ, and shut down my senses
one by one, but all the short night long
some friendly software
plays dreams of you:

coming dazzling from your sun-bath,
dressing up for out with the starry sky
in evening dress, or down
for a night in with me.
What are dreams for else, when
winning love we win the risk of losing?
Keep smiling and walking past;
let me celebrate this longing.

SINGING TODAY

Comet with white nightdress flying,
the startling. That's the universe,
and so is this *Good Bird Guide*
I'm about to show to this woman
who is also the universe.
And today is the day. Not that yesterday
belongs to people and places
I regret and would rather forget,
though she is none of them
Can you hear the singing bird?

Nor that so little is worth remembering,
though she is most of it, and more
with each astounding sun.
Today's the day because the chances
of our meeting in the multi-storey
in one of those collisions not covered
by insurance, or of her
standing here this morning
by this open window on the garden
Can you hear the springbird singing?

Or of life on any star system
anywhere, are ten to the power
of 40,000 to one against,
which means that every time we kiss
—and each time is the first time ever
since nothing happens twice—
I win every lottery in the universe,
first prize, bingo, jackpot,
jillpot if you like, life, love, the lot.
Can you hear me singing, bird?

THINKING OF YOU

I spent last night burning all your letters.
Today I stray from room to room and try
to remember your last address, and whether
I promised your faithful hamster would die

smashed against the walls, which incidentally
are magnolia now, magnolia all the way
because you loathed it. And environmentally
sound, undyed toilet rolls have had their day.

My trolley shrieks with rolls of every hue:
apricot, strawberry, peach. I like to think
that when, in your memory, I flush the loo,
gradually a warm, suggestive pink
will spread across the long, cold miles of sea,
and you will look at it, and think of me.

POETRY

He came home drunk,
late and dysfunctional, and she cried,
'You don't love me. Waist down
you hate me, you bastard.'
But being a poet
he took rejection in his stride
and when she gashed her breasts
with a steak knife and screamed,
'Make bloody poetry out of that,'
he did, the bastard.

HERO'S WELCOME

Mrs. Odysseus had had enough.
Nineteen years he'd been gone, gadding about
in the Med and she in the dark without
so much as a postcard. And it was tough,

being rich and besieged by suitors, and
by years. Hard-pressed, she undertook to pick
the hopeful who pulled off a party trick
once flaunted by her ex. Eros was banned.

And the winner? Her erstwhile long-lost mate,
who, though embarrassed by the fecklessness
of her decision making processes,
played ball. Every Odysseus, home late,
no real excuse, expects to face a test,
or, in less heroic times, an inquest.

DIVORCE PARTY

Rabbi Hillel, glad you could make it. Here, allow me.
Yes, Mike's farewell to Kylie, the decree absolute
celebrations. No big deal, not these days, their splitting up,
though they always moved so well together. It wasn't
that they didn't love each other, still do, I suspect,
and it wasn't that his bony wooden furniture,
stiff with knobs and knuckles, attacked her swelling billows
of upholstered foam when the place was empty. Or
that no two people are the same and no one person
is the same twice. Or that she was a feeler and he
a thinker, a feeling thinker, he thought, as she felt
herself a thinking feeler. They were, as like as not,
but it wasn't that. And snow-white feet was right, they froze
his kidneys in the midnight hours, but it wasn't that,
or that he was boring and she an inconstant nymph:
Eve, 'Lila, Mandy Magdalene, Ruth, and Jezebel
in a single morning, the illusory stasis
of cornstack hair and pitchfork tail keeping him ducking
and heaving before he left for the office breathless.
Absurd when you think about it, which you had better not—
or he wields his long naked sword and she slides open
her drawerful of little knives and, at the point where
being human is less important than being right,
neither wins uncut. Or they make up from the waist down,
bodies remembering what brains forget, and then Mike,
that's Mike under the table because it's his party,
lets the broth boil over. As you famously said, Rabbi,
a wife can be put away if she lets the broth boil
over ... The husband's proximity to the pot's not
morally material? Well, perhaps you have been
simmering rather a long time. Here, let me tempt you
with a slice of the cake. Some time ago—two thousand
years?—you taught that love's beaming lighthouse trips out
when the symbolic broth symbolically boils over
the matrimonial cooker, signifying gross
breach of trust, lust gone bad, love gone bust, the usual

[51]

impossibles. Let me get you another champagne.
Was it like this in your day, Rabbi Hillel, in Israel,
the broth boiling over on every side? It was?
Mike will find that reassuring when he surfaces,
and consoling as well. He'll be sorry he missed you.

JUST CHURCHES

The insurance agent I had come to see
and the antique shop next door I hadn't
were closed for lunch. Even the chintzy café
was Closed For Lunch. A heavy drizzle, slightly
short of pattering, kept Barton steeping,
but St. Mary's was open, empty and there,
and so was I. She took me in: that peace,
the laid-to-restfulness of entombed centuries,
which recoiled when a bolt of lightning hit
the sanctuary, backed up with a show-stopping
'Oh, shit!' normally inaudible at the altar.
A second flash. I had begun to pray that
my life insurance covered acts of God,
when a rotund Norman pillar was elbowed
aside by a burly prophet bearing a tripod,
flash-gun, and pendulous with small black boxes.

'Hello! I thought I was here on my own.
I didn't disturb you,' he hoped,
and shuffled his equipment uncomfortably.
'You see, I didn't really ought
to be here; I'm not into religion, just churches.
Old woodwork, joinery, if you like,
from way back when carpenter was king.'
I wished I'd thought of that, and turned
to see the door swing unlatched in the wind
to admit a grey ghosting of
King Carpenter's descendants carrying planks,
or wearing Burberrys and cameras.

'Don't know much about Christ and that.
Carpenter wasn't he? From Galilee
or somewhere, not from Grimsby like me.
I bet he would have liked this roof:
each beam and rafter from rugged oak;
the joints. The strength lies in the joints,

male and female, mortice and tenon,
tongue and groove, half lap, double cogg.
I could go on,' he broke off, eyes
drawn into the upturned, dark hull
of the roof, and frowned. 'Trouble is,
the best joints can't be seen from the floor.'
He gestured aloft with a smart
zoom lens, noticed it and confided
'Redundancy money,' hitching his Pentax.
'But just imagine those poor sods
toiling away, only to leave
their personal best hidden from sight
like so much rubbish. They were told
that God could see it: that's what mattered!'
His laugh was loud enough to wake
the dead, who caught and knocked it wall
to wall until it fell to dust.
His 'Great acoustics' was a whisper.
'They don't build like this any more:
all regulations, British Standards,
Codes of Practice, no honest craftsmanship.'
He Englished his disgust into
'God, I need a pint.' Then, 'Anyway,
nice to have met you, and remember,'
twinkling like a chisel, 'when
and if you die, first thing you'll need
is a carpenter.' He turned,
and banged out whistling like a lark,
before it sees the dark shape hovering.

THE RAIDERS

The gang comes gunning along
the front, makes a barricade of spokes,
cuts its engines and struts about,
lights up, and cracks open its Cokes.
The heads unshelled from helmets
are hair-free and pink. Black leather
peels back to show white beards.

Unsaddled and unmasked, the raiders
individualise, kneel to admire
one another's bikes and joke with
a small punk wife who has retained
her figure (bra, jeans, pants and away!),
or one of the bikers' daughters maybe,
40 years old and safely pillioned.

Once they would have rampaged
through town to where the bathing huts
stand ankle deep in cream seas.
Now they keep on the right side
of wrong, and go as far as they can
without having to come back
to haunt the having been here.

Down the road they go, the Boys,
accoutred for the battle against age,
polished machines well tuned
and responsive between their legs,
roaring off to lurking pile-ups,
breakdowns and unfinished journeys:
Hell's Angels who have outlived

their uselessness and become
no more unfit for heaven than any.
But we who have more past
than future must avoid thinking

we must avoid going down that road,
for they are not like us, how we
see ourselves, and neither are we.

COGITO

Skiving men, mostly, parked equidistantly
along the shore to read Sunday's papers,
where a shallow elevation of the eye
douses overheated stocks and shares
in millions of water, retreat before the coaches.

The daytrippers come for the getting away
as much as for the uninterrupted air and sky,
and their gait is the giveaway: pairs in shoes
not meant for stepping higher than a kerb
or farther than a nearby burger bar, sore feet
a small price to pay for being alive, here, today.

Oh cogito I do like to be,
to be myself beside the sea. I do
so like to be beside myself with you
at the sea, beside myself at the sea
with you beside me. Oh I do, ergo sum.

And who would epistemologically dare
to doubt either of these two radiant pairs
of false teeth in careworn faces,
now sharing a radiant, bipartite smile
with a world in which they might as well not,

beside the unthinking and therefore nonexistent
sea. They enjoy themselves when they're here,
when ever, and whatever makes him tick,
her tock, sets them chiming on the sea wall
above the darkly advancing surf,
killing time before the long journey back.

You can come out now, they've gone; each brief,
debatable life has been transferred.
And the local goodwives, mostly, here today,
here tomorrow and evidentially unreal,
tut-tut alone among the leavings
and unleash their lapdogs on the beach.

SEA COAL

Down first thing for a breakfast of air
by the sea, where far-off oilskinned
figures dig for bloodworms. While here
a long black tidemark defines
the sea's jurisdiction on land.
An old couple, long winter coats
thrumming in the wind, trudge the line,
bent double for nuggets of coal
no bigger than Oxo cubes. Finally,
in a plastic bag slaked with sand,
they have amassed a shovelful.
I hope they get their drudgery's worth:
a firelit hearth, perhaps: warm hands
at bedtime to touch each other with.

COLORADO DESERT NIGHT

Swatted twice by the selfsame billboard
with 'Gotta long standin' problem, buster?
Try kneelin',' I stopped to ask how
to get the hell out of there before dark,
and then I heard it, the unearthly silence.

Two unfallen kids hanging from a new
old rugged cross outside the mission,
not by their necks but by their hands,
heard it and dangled awestruck,
and the elderly cowboys praying inside,
'Give us a break. Dear Lord, give us
a break,' were exalted by it: the Earth
holding its breath, the audible quiet.

Sound, having nothing to strike or blow,
had gone away. A presence (some said
an absence) raised itself just beyond
the edge of human consciousness
(which is of course the very epitome
of existence (so much for existence)),
we explained variously and at length,
and chiefly to ourselves. But how absurd
is the word compared to the silence of God.

And when the thin plainsong resumed,
a wandering tune of dustblown badlands,
we upped the volume and fell to dancing,
kissing, fighting, writing poems, anything
to blot out that stillness. And I knew
I could never leave there with this unsaid,

not with the desert sky darkening over us
and the great inanimates gathering round,
wondering what we are, and how much
longer we need to surrender and join them
in their deathly shining.

INSPECTOR OF TIDES

Conditions were ideal, grey scarves of cloud
breezing off-shore to muffle
the high gold cirrus that day had left behind.
The light was draining down,
but if it went he had his torch for pitfalls
after nightfall and his compass
for unscrambling fogbanks stranded ashore.
A redundant accountant
flounders until he lights on something that needs
measuring more
than 1,440 empty minutes a day
month after month,
quantifying his bitterness, his scrap value,
his wife's tenderness.

What he discovered and what, like all discoveries,
had always been there,
was the overlooked redundancy of sea,
approximately 920 metres—
paced out one sleepless night—from his front door,
coming and going at leisure.
When the in-laws came visiting he invited them
to stroll by the sea,
to find it gone, shoved off to a shrivelled line.
They stopped going,
and shortly afterwards they had stopped coming.

He took to idly clocking it
in and out, between the theme park and the mouth
of a nameless beck,
one of those places only the sea remembers.
But after the last biannual high,
a ragged sea running, ramming the sea wall,
shunting sandbanks about,
charged with filling every valley, bringing low
every mountain and hill,

and smoothing the rough until there is no earth
left on Earth,
he knew he had half the picture, the daytripper's
snapshot from the prom:
he needed the other half, the unphotographed lows
held posed
in their extreme positions. Here was a vacancy,
shift work involved,
punctuality imperative. Being the only applicant,
he got the job.

The sea, having no shape of its own,
or colour either,
fills every emptiness to the gills. Four times a day,
including nights,
he checks the sea against its own great clock.
High tides happen near home,
newspapers publish the best times to catch him,
our newfound man,
unusually bronzed, long-haired and two stone lighter,
but low tides
are the sea lurching home to bed; they lure him out
past sandbanks,
water ditches and away, sometimes for hours,
sometimes in a seafog's
vaporous clinging or battered by gales of darkness.

Twice daily he treks
to the low tideline across a communal sunbed,
basking or pursuing
flabby beachballs into a tinkling surf,
or strides across
an icy sand-blasted desert to catch the tide
when it pauses
to fill its aqueous lung before turning back
to dispute the beach,
the tilting ground's long slope where the land
is lapped and overlapped,

a combat zone of empty shells and castles
built by city kids,
where the boundaries are endlessly fought out.

In the now receding town,
his desk is empty, dead files repose in long
undrawn metal drawers,
their square mouths rusting shut; and ex-colleagues
balance numbers
he trusted, once, and calculate for all their lives
are worth,
blindly reducing a world of grand designs
to a rubble of figures.
Some afternoons when our screens are blank
we think of him,
patrolling the borders in the dead of night,
hair streaming, chin set,
to see how far he can go, how far away
he can get
from his old accountable, rejected self.
He needs no reason,
the point is if it isn't pointless he might as well
be elsewhere
pleasing someone, anyone, and being useful.
No thought
of drowned forests, sunk islands with bells tolling
and MPs in Westminster,
or loot of combs and pins of bone or horn.
Driven by purpose
and intentionality for years, the pointlessness
is pure and irresistible.

At today's low-water, the sea rolls back a mile
to become mainly sky
mirroring the tides of air on their long migrations,
quits that strip of land
it squats on 12 months out of 12, bar turning time
(as determined by wind force

and quarter, surge and pressure, and the moon),
and assembles
for a soft exploratory skirmish. The moon
was another find,
drawing oceans towards it and letting go
in gravity's game
of physical attraction without union:
the slow subsonic drumming.

The light holds, and the lowest low, the limit
of the moon's ambition
discloses a seabed never seen before,
his alone to note
the banks of a lost dyke burrowing eastwards,
half-buried sculptures
the sea has licked into mindless forms,
where no dryshod foot
but his has ever stood. And this transient place
carries the stamp
and insignia of his newly-discovered feet
when it goes under,
maybe for ever. Before he turns with the tide
to recross a foreshore
become more home than home, he photographs
the fugitive land.
He'll show you last year's, enlarged and framed;
he'll show you nothing else,
and you'll look, and look, till you feel the tide
trembling at the threshold,
warning you to escape to higher ground.